"Hush, devil, who speaks so!"

"The Red Knight speaks that way,
   He who fucks everyday!"

for Vasko Popa

"Daniel, qu'as tu fait de tes lions?"

Vuk Stefanović Karadžić

Red Knight

Serbian Women's Songs

edited and translated by
Daniel Weissbort and Tomislav Longinovic

introduced by Tomislav Longinovic

with a preface by Charles Simic

illustrations and artist's afterword by
Audrey Jones

translator's afterword by Daniel Weissbort

Menard Press/
King's College London
1992

RED KNIGHT:
Serbian Women's Songs

Translation and essays © 1992:
Daniel Weissbort and Tomislav Longinovic

Preface © 1992: Charles Simic

Illustrations © 1992: Audrey Jones

Illustrator's afterword © 1992: Audrey Jones

Cover design: Merlin James

Distribution in America:
SPD Inc
1814 San Pablo Avenue
Berkeley, CA 94702, USA

ISBN: 0 9513753 4 2

THE MENARD PRESS
8 The Oaks
Woodside Avenue
London N12 8AR
081-446-5571

KING'S COLLEGE LONDON
Strand, London WC2R 2LS

Typeset by Wendy Pank
Printed by The Iceni Press
Book production by Fakenham Photosetting Limited

Contents

*Note that the Serbian originals begin on page 87

7

Charles Simic

Preface

When my father's father, who came from a line of village blacksmiths, wanted to upset my mother, who was a member of an old and distinguished Belgrade family, he would take some well-known Serbian heroic ballad and turn it around. So, instead of Prince Marko going out early one morning to fight Turks, he would lose his drawers and spend the rest of the day looking for them. These improvised parodies appalled my mother and delighted my grandfather and father. I was caught in between. I tried my best to keep a straight face.

The songs in this collection echo the heroic ballads and the short lyrics in that tradition. They employ familiar narrative strategies and literary conceits for similarly subversive ends. My mother, who was not a prude, found such irreverence shocking. "Some things are sacred," she'd say, and who could argue with that? The traditional ballads and songs are works of great delicacy of feeling. They are the pride of Serbian people. How could one possibly make fun of them?

Middle-class city dwellers, like my mother, are always surprised by the realities of folk life and culture. I remember a Paris-educated cousin of ours claiming once that Serbian peasants never use bad language. His reasoning went like this: The country folk must be angelically pure, since they are the moral foundation of our people.

Even at the age of ten I knew better, since I spent summers in my grandfather's village playing with the children my cousin romanticized.

"Sonny-boy, Milutine,
What's that hanging down your thighs?"

the little girls sang as I walked by turning red in the face. Sober minds, tender souls, schoolteachers, policemen, priests would all shout in a chorus that this is in no way representative of the Serbian people! They are the very ones, of course, who prohibited the publication of this collection for almost two hundred years.

It's the revenge of the yokels, this collection is. The peasant story-tellers – and this is true in all cultures – do not just tell their tales and sing their songs to be amusing. There's an undercurrent of realism, of spite, especially in comic pieces. Tragedy is a cosmic matter; comedy concerns individual lives in their dailiness. These poems tell us more about how Serbian peasants actually lived than many of the heroic and lyric songs.

For instance, to give a single example, till very recently in rural households everybody slept in one bed. I saw it with my own eyes when I was a child. Grownups and children and even guests climbed into the same huge bed. What went on under the heavy covers anyone can imagine. There were no mysteries of sex, even for the smallest child.

That everything comes down to the body is

the wisdom of the comic and the erotic. You can talk all you want about heroes and saints and the rest, but in the end it's the belly and the reproductive organs that matter. Truth is naked and laughing. Women, as these songs prove, always knew that better than men.

The tradition is old, of course. The ribaldry of medieval carnivals and feasts and trickster tales everywhere is part of it. We find it also in early American blues:

"Your nuts hang down like a damn church clapper,
And your dick stands up like a steeple,"

sings one Bessie Jackson.

The joys of good sex and the failure of men to perform adequately are the subject of both. "Fucking is a thing that will take me to heaven," says Jackson. There are many Serbian counterparts to this.

"I thought, Mama,
I was going to fly."

Sex is exhilarating and hilarious. Come to think of it, there's nothing more funny than sex, if you ask these folk.

There are darker overtones, too, in these songs. Incest and especially rape are frequent. Beware of priests and monks especially, the songs are saying. All these pious hypocrites, mumblers of Holy Masses, and snatchers of poor people's coins, are dangerous. We are in a world of drunkards, gluttons and horny devils masquerading as Christians. The laughter, at times, is ambivalent, derisive and terrified.

Still, merriment prevails. Mainly, these are

songs in praise of the erotic. They delight in the body and its appetites and rejoice in our human foolishness. They bring us good cheer the world's horrors and deceits could not silence.

Tomislav Longinovic

When the Body Sings Itself

The songs that comprise this collection were re-
corded in the XIX century by Vuk Stefanović
Karadžić, a Serbian man of letters of humble origins
whose pioneering work as a linguist, translator,
ethnographer and collector of oral tradition laid
the foundation for the emergence of modern Ser-
bian literature and culture. Besides the already
celebrated heroic epics that flourished in the Bal-
kans during the long centuries of Ottoman domina-
tion, Vuk collected a wide variety of proverbs,
lyrics, laments and riddles that characterized both
the life of the Serbs who lived in occupied Serbia
and those who lived scattered in Croatia, Bosnia
and Hungary. He divided this material into two
groups. The first group consisted of songs sung by
a man accompanying himself on a *gusle*, a one-
stringed instrument played with a bow, these being
the heroic songs; the other group Vuk called *wom-
en's* songs, which he believed to be far older and
originating in the ancient Slavic country beyond
the Carpathian Mountains. He gathered and pub-
lished all these folk creations in the four collections
which have since become the basis of the contem-
porary Serbian literary canon.

But besides those four "legitimate" collections,
Vuk recorded a fifth one of women's songs, which
was preserved only in manuscript and which he

never tried to publish. This "fifth" collection of so-called obscene (*bezobrazne*) songs, dealt with those aspects of peasant life which would probably have shocked and alienated the exiled Serbian élite in Hungary, very much under the sway of the Serbian Orthodox Church. It is likely that Vuk did not want to compromise himself by publishing this sexually explicit material, which was bound to confirm and reinforce the prejudices that his powerful enemies had already nurtured. Metropolitan Stratimirovic, one of the fiercest opponents of Vuk's linguistic reforms (which replaced the Serbian version of Church Slavonic with vernacular speech), had already accused the self-taught Vuk of trying to pollute national literary traditions with the base language of "swineherds and cowgirls." Vuk, inspired by the Romantic search for authentic cultural roots among the common folk, resisted these pressures, believing that his Serbian compatriots would soon come to realize that the vernacular language was an incomparable force for the enlightenment of the illiterate peasant masses. History proved that Vuk's cultural politics were more suited to the times than the medieval hegemony the Church attempted to maintain over all spheres of Serbian learning.

Although the Orthodox faith was not as repressive and politicized as the Catholic, it rested on the same Christian dogmas regarding the Satanic origin of sexual desire. The Serbian aristocracy, which had accepted Orthodox Christianity in 864 AD, partially assimilated this view of sexuality as an external and evil force which had to be channeled through the marital relationship, if not altogether eliminated. However, for the great majority of peasants, the pre-Christian belief system, regarding the body and its functions as an extension of nature and the elements, was only superficially affected by this disembodied vision of sexuality. The fertility of Mother Earth was to be ensured by sympathetic magic, through a variety of ritual acts which included singing, dancing and sex. Some of the songs in this collection are undoubtedly poetic echoes of those pagan times, when the bodies of men and women had their place in a larger, cosmic, sexual order.

What was the nature of these rituals, most of which occurred around the summer solstice? It is hard to say, since the only surviving source texts are of Christian origin, and a negative attitude towards the pagan practices prevails. Ethnographic data on Balkan peasant life, however, might help us reconstruct their meaning. One of the prominent features of Balkan folklore is the dance known as the *kolo* (round dance). At the start, the male and female dancers are usually separated, in columns of equal length, facing each other. It is during this initial stage of the dance that the boys and girls tease each other as to their appearance, habits and dancing skills. As the *kolo* progresses and the dancers begin to warm up, the songs become bolder, touching directly on the sexuality of partners. It may be assumed that these songs and dances were a prelude to ritual sexual activity. The shorter poems in this collection, like "The Lass" and "What I'll Give for a Real Man," (also known as *poskocice*, from the verb 'to jump up' i.e. 'to be startled'), belong to this category.

The longer ones, like "Granny Todorina" and "Mummy's Milya", on the other hand, are parodic elaborations of the Serbian heroic epic, similar to those that Charles Simic remembers his grandfather singing. They are sung in *desterac* (decasyllabics) but without *gusle* and with a mixed rather than all-male audience, as in the solemn, dramatic performances of the epic. Using the same formulaic de-vices, the female singer substitutes for the mace (*buzdovan*) or the swift sword (*britka sablja*) of the epic hero, the hardened piece of excrement that Granny Todorina uses as a weapon to strike dead shepherd Zvekan's bitch (p83). This scatological attitude scorns the elevated discourse of war, elic-iting instead laughter which dethrones the heroes of the epic bards. This is a laughter that originates in the lower part of the body and questions all the norms of morality, religion or politics professed by the upper part. The humour of these longer songs constitutes an instinctual critique of everything that is conventional, petrified and didactic in the culture.

Folk laughter opposes itself to the patriarchal social order and expresses the anarchic, carni-valesque reversal of accepted values. Thus, priests and monks are portrayed as the apostles of lechery, a clear sign that the common folk understands very well the double standards characteristic of ruling class morality. The male sexual organ bears an aristocratic title (*crven ban* or 'red knight'), not only because it has the privilege of daily copulation (*crven ban koji jebe svaki dan* or "the red knight who fucks every day"), but also because all noblemen are demeaned by such a personification. By using obscene language, folk singers do not arouse sexual passions, so much as provoke a belly laughter that mocks the established social order and the constraints it places on the body. The above-mentioned *kolo* dance provides a space within which pagan attitudes can return in full force and affirm the simple and comical truths of the body, while challenging the exalted spirit of clerical prohibition.

The immediacy with which the Serbian original addresses the native speaker is shocking and exhilarating at the same time, any initial uneasiness being quickly replaced by laughter, offensive only to those moralists who prevented the publication of this collection in Yugoslavia before the 1970's. Since then, there have been over ten editions and the collection has become a best-seller. Pop musicians have used the lyrics to produce hit-singles, reintroducing this material into the urban culture of Belgrade, which had fought so hard to detach itself from its rustic origins. The truth of the body conveyed by these women's songs is a powerful antidote to the poison of the nationalist rhetoric presently being disseminated by (male) politicians in Yugoslavia. I hope that this irreverent spirit will prevail in a country whose reckless leaders, in their tragi-comical pursuit of power at any price, have brought its peoples to the brink of self-destruction. These songs mock the seriousness and deadliness of such heroic pretentions, celebrating instead a realm where joy and laughter not only reveal the wisdom of the body, but also expose the illusory and tragic nature of all power.

University of Wisconsin-Madison
August, 1991

Serbian Women's Songs

Spite

The girl said to her friend: "I swear,
On my brother's life, betrothed I'll never be;
But if they force me to, I swear,
On my brother's life, wed I'll never be;
But if they force me to, I swear,
On my brother's life, lie with him I'll never;
But if they force me to, I swear,
On my brother's life, he'll not put it in;
But if they force me to, I swear,
On my brother's life, he shall not take it
        out!"

A Wager

This is what an unwed lad once said
To the girl he fancied in his bed:
"My sweet, let's lay a wager, you and me,
Let's wager on your necklace and my horse
That we shall sleep together one whole
      night
And, never touching, lie there side by side!"
No sooner said than done, they went to bed.
But scarcely had the midnight hour struck,
Than the girl said to her companion:
"Turn your face to me, my brave lad, turn,
Or may your mother turn your lifeless
      corpse!
Take me in your arms, or may they waste
      away!
Kiss me on the lips, or may your lips go bad!
Bite me hard, or may your teeth fall out!"

Young Hero

They were dancing in the village,
Our young hero in the circle,
A long sheepskin to his girdle
And a short prick to his kneebone.
When our men saw what he'd got there,
They began to talk it over,
And they came to a decision:
'Make his coat a little longer,
Take a little off his pecker!"
When our women overheard them,
They addressed our village headmen:
"You can take some off his sheepskin,
But you may not touch his pecker,
Or with us you'll have to reckon!"

Not The Grass

A girl was picking violets in the field.
The long grass pricked her pussy as she
    knelt.
It wasn't grass, it was a prick she felt!

The Best Place For The Village

Let us move the village, friends!
Where shall we move the village, where?
Between the eyebrows of a girl.
You can't have a village there:
There's no river, there's no wood,
There's no earth to cultivate.

Let us move the village, friends!
Where shall we move the village, where?
Between the two breasts of a girl.
You can't have a village there:
There's no river, there's no wood,
There's no earth to cultivate.

Let us move the village, friends!
Where shall we move the village, where?
Between the two legs of a girl:
Yes, you can have a village there.
There's a river, there's a wood,
There is earth to cultivate.

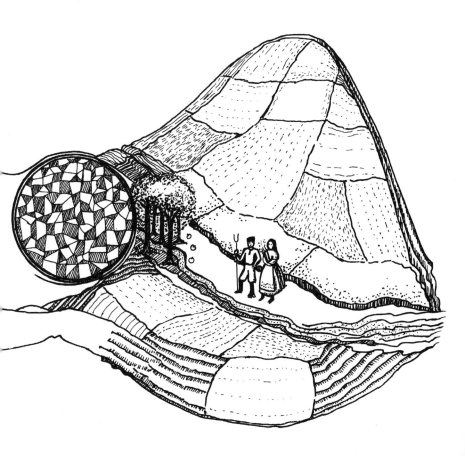

To His Girl

O my love, my very own,
When I see your tits I moan,
And my pants drop on their own.

A Lass

She sweeps the roadway clear,
Arse up in the air.
You can see her twat,
She's proud of what she's got.

Neither Paradise Nor The End

One day a girl was shinning up a prick,
To catch a glimpse of paradise from it,
Either paradise or the pecker's end.
She lost her grip then, and her right foot
    slipped.
The girl cursed her right foot right royally:
"Fuck you right foot, and shaft, fuck you
    as well.
You slipped and, me, I didn't get to see!"

Gathering Wood

Mama sent me off
To gather firewood,
But there came, mama,
An unwed lad;
And he started, mama,
To rub my tummy,
And I thought, mama,
He would give me some pants;
And when he started, mama,
To rub my navel,
I thought, mama,
He would give me a sash;
And when he started, mama,
To lift up my legs,
I thought, mama,
He would give me some socks;
But when he started, mama,
To stick it in my cunt,
I thought, mama,
I was going to die;
And when he started, mama,
To spill his pearls,
I thought, mama,
I was going to fly!

What I'll Give For A Real Man!

Two black jades I shall give
For a man to share my crib,
And a grey, if I'm in luck,
For a lad who can really fuck!

Feeble Ranko

Last night his mama married Ranko off,
Bitterly the maid laments and curses:
"Damn any miserable mother who
Lands a horny girl with a feeble man!
The stars are fading and I am still a
      maiden!
May the one who married me eat shit,
May his hands fall off, if he doesn't lift my
        legs,
May the flocking crows crap on his prick!"

A Damned Shame!

It makes me wild, my lover's such a child,
He can't kiss, just wants to play the fool.
He rolls me in the dirt, and messes up my
        skirt,
It's quite a sight, four layers of pearly white!
I thought I'd embroider a scarf for my
        dear one –
The way he kisses, he'd never wear one!

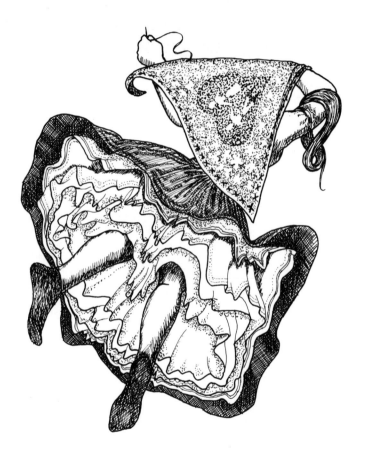

How Can She Spin?

The new bride makes a fearful din:
If she's not screwed, how can she spin!
Either fuck her or take her home to mother,
Let her mama's lover fuck her!

Boy And Girl

"Girl, wiggle your arse!"
"And you, brother, your moustache!"

Astonished

I'm astonished, it's a sin
How the cunt keeps water in:
There's no bottom, there's no hoop,
There's no spigot, there's no top.
If barrel-making was my role
I would love to mend that hole.

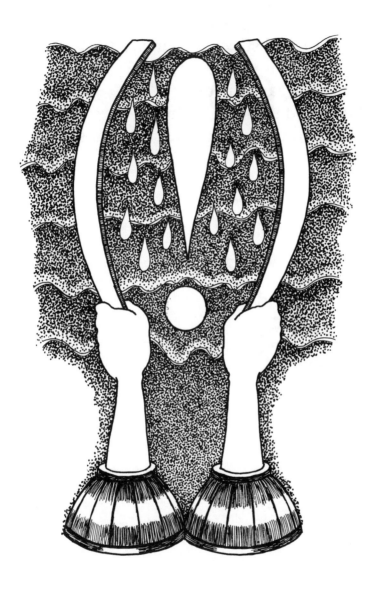

I Was Dumbstruck

I was dumbstruck and amazed
That the cunt never grazed,
But it began to peel.
It peeled those little plums –
Come on, then, let's fuck her gums!

After The Wedding

When I was a little girl, God knows,
I couldn't even piss on my own.
But, thank you Lord, I'm married now,
I lift my legs and the waters run!

The Priest And The Girl

The priest took the girl firmly by the hand,
Led her to the shed, laid her on the stand,
Then he put his priest's hat over her head,
And he whispered softly in her ear:
"I'll just untie your dress, my dear, and soon
My prick will come to you all on its own!"

A Funny Holy Man

Oh mother, what a funny holy man –
First he fucks you, then hears your
    confession,
First lifts your legs, then listens to your sins!

Underneath The Hawthorn

My mother sent me to the woods
To gather berries where I could.
The woods were overflowing with every
Kind of berry, smooth or hairy.
Ah, poor wretch, I was so famished,
I began to climb a hawthorn.
But my foot slipped and I fell from
Hawthorn top to hawthorn bottom,
Where a lad happened to be.
I fell on top of him and he –
"Whose knee's pressing hard on me?"
I slipped beneath him, shyly breathing:
"I rode you, now it's your turn to!"

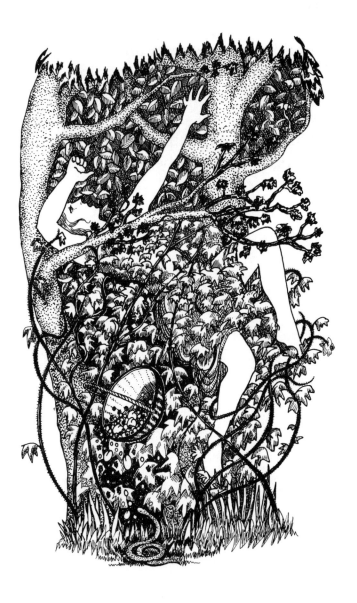

Selling The Meadow

My daddy has a meadow and some woods,
I'd sell them for a dollar if I could,
To buy myself a skirt named lays-you-
down,
And an apron, flips-up-on-its own,
And stockings, strip-them-off-
        and-stick-it-in!

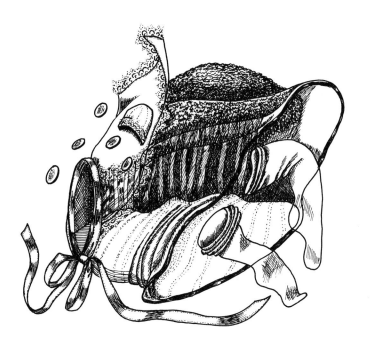

Oh, The Guest!

Every bird sings sweetly –
But blackbird's best! Blackbird's best!
And the host fucks featly –
But, oh, the guest! Oh, the guest!

Now What!

The monks are haymaking between the
      hill crests,
The girls are hugging jugs between their
      breasts.
"Come on, fathers, here's cool water for you!"
One of the monks then broke his prick in
      two.
So they took it to a blacksmith at his forge,
The blacksmith whacked it, cracked it,
      now what!
They took it to a goldsmith then to plate it,
He plated it, prick paid for it, so now what!
They took it to a witch to work her magic,
The old dame chanted, pecker panted,
      now what!
They took it to a locksmith to secure it,
The locksmith hurt it, pecker spurted,
      now what!

Pickles

Give me a pussy and some pepper,
And I'll make pickles for the pecker!

The Friar

The friar tripped on a sod and fell.
He broke the prick that fucks so well.
Married or betrothed, the women
Gathered round and stared at him:
"Oh, our cunts' pride, oh holy friar,
 Is this a sign of heaven's ire!"

Mother And Daughter

"Mother, mother, the monk wakes me
    at night.
He wakes and kisses me between the eyes.
Do you think, mother, should I kiss him
    back?"
"Kiss him, my daughter, kiss him and be
    damned!
Why when your mother was your age,
    my pet,
By morning she'd had nine of them in bed,
And number ten was your very own dad–
And in her spare time she wove a rug
    as well!"

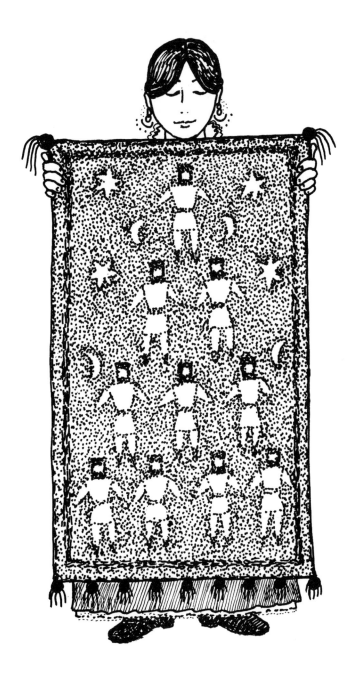

We Will Go To The Fair

Cunt is cooking carp tonight,
Prick is watching with delight.
Cunt picks up a shovel, swings it,
Swipes prick on the neck with it.
Prick begins to cry and moan,
Pussy tries to calm him down:
"Hush, my pricklet, don't be scared,
Tomorrow is St Vitus' Day.
Tomorrow we'll go to the fair,
We'll buy a silken ribbon there,
Ribbon for a pecker's neck."

A Rotten Neighbour

The pussy and the arse were quarreling.
The arse whispered softly to the pussy:
"You're a rotten neighbour, a proper pest,
I'm fed up with your never-ending
        guests –
They screw you and they flog me with
        their balls!"

Another's Tart

Hey ho, don't lose heart,
Don't befriend another's tart:
This could prove your great mistake,
He'll grab your prick and wring its neck!

To The Clump

Hey-ho, let us go
To the clump where they hump!

Telling By Her Eyes

You can tell – it isn't luck –
The girl who wants to fuck.
Look around and there's your prize,
Gazing at you with wide eyes.

Prayer

May God grant that my lover never can't!

The Turkish Women
and Vuk From The Woods

When the Turkish women were out digging,
Bread and pies were brought them for
    their dinner,
And a little cask of sweet red wine –
Afterwards they smacked their lips and slept.
From out the woods crept Vuk on hands
    and knees,
And screwed the Turkish women
    three times each.
When the women woke up from their
    dreams,
The bey's young wife got to her feet
    and spoke:
"Have we not drunk sweet wine before
    and yet
Our pants, my dear friends, never were
    so wet!
Let's strip the barrel, girls, then each of us
Can take a stave and sound her
    pitch-black cunt."
And so they stripped the barrel, took a stave,
And each one found she was two
    stave-lengths deep,
Except the bey's young wife was
    three to four!

Old Boy And Old Dame

In the cold and drizzling rain,
The old boy's shelling the old dame.
On a tree trunk, in the meadow,
It's hard work for him to bed her!

A Proposal

Let me, oh my darling, do,
Make a bagpipe out of you.
Let me push my pipe in
When I've finished dining!

Caution

Considering the cunt is neighbour
To the arsehole, brother, take care,
In the middle of the night,
Keep your eyes peeled or you might
Miss your mark – instead of quim,
Fill the other to the rim.

For A Ducat

Sweep the chimney, flames go up it,
Kate won't fuck without a ducat.
Here's one ducat for my Kata,
Now I'm sure she'll let me fuck her!
Give her two, she'll fuck you,
Give her three, she'll fuck me,
Give her four, she'll fuck more!

Trouble

Oh, poor you, just look how big
Is our Miodrag's red prick!
If, poor you, you gave your all,
There'd be spunk from wall to wall!

Friends, I tell you, that's a trifle –
Look at Pishta's, get an eyeful:
He drags his huge prick behind him –
God, if he'd only put it in!

Vema

Dawn is breaking,
Unforsaken,
Vema dozes,
As prick noses.

The Blacksmith And His Wife

The blacksmith hammers, his
    sweet wife sighs,
His naked ballocks are all eyes.

Even Grandpop

Even grandpop
Gets his end up,
Like a billy,
Occasionally.
The vein so prized
By womankind
Still fills out nicely,
If not quite nightly.

Got Her!

I sowed broad beans and melon seeds,
And the girl stopped by to see,
To pick the melons, peck the beans.
One night I waited up for her,
Waited up till she was there,
Slipped my hand inside her bodice,
Where I found two cucumbers,
Neither under ripe nor over,
Just the right amount for nibbling,
Moved my hand a little lower,
Just below her belly-button –
Below her button, popped the melon,
And from the melon water flowed.
I led my stallion to the water,
And hard was it to leave thereafter.

When They Join A Boy And A Girl
(In Dalmatia and Bosnia)

Evening to you, oh my brother,
Here she is, your well-beloved –
Turn her well, oh my brother,
Row her well, oh my brother,
Three or four times before dawn,
So the brothers don't poke fun!
Before you stretches the dark woods,
In the woods a she-bear smoulders,
Black braid shaggy on her shoulders;
You draw out your battle spear,
With it pin the great she-bear
Through the throat, as she stands there!
Grab her by the fore part, brother,
There two cukes you will discover;
And below the belly-button,
There you'll find a bursting melon!

Boy And Girl

A fir I planted in a high place,
Every day I brought it water;
I sent a girl to care for it,
And I thought that's what she'd do;
But then slumber overtook her,
So I sent a boy to wake her,
And I thought that's what he'd do;
One of her fair legs he lifted,
And I thought he wants to dig;
Then he lifted up the other,
And I thought he wants to plough;
He began to rub her belly,
And I thought he wants to hoe;
He pulled off her little dress,
And I thought, a flag he's raising;
He untied her underpants,
And I thought he wants to sow;
When he pulled out his fine capstan,
Now, I thought, he wants to dream.

Trickster

By the icy waters of the river
A peasant girl was bleaching sheets one day.
The snowy linen lay there almost dry,
When a trickster lad passed by that way,
And tramped across the girl's sheets on
      the ground.
She wept and then she cursed him angrily:
"God grant your crops should wither on
      the stalk!"
But tugging his moustache, the
      trickster said:
"May my wheat grow as thick as this
      moustache,
And may the drought not touch it any time!"
But she was trickier than the lad, that girl –
She seized hold of her two breasts with
      her hands:
"May hailstones large and round as these
      descend
And flatten all your wheat stalks to
      the ground,
So that their thickness will not help at all!"
Then to the peasant girl the trickster said,
As he slid his hand still lower down:
"May my ears of wheat be big as this,
So that the hailstones cannot damage them!"

But the girl was trickier than the lad.
She grabbed hold of herself then lower down
And to the lad she whispered softly now:
"May crows as big as this flock in your field,
And may they gobble all your ears of wheat!"
Which having said, they fell upon each other.

Young Kokan

The evil hour, the day, the hungry year,
Master Kokan rued, when he engaged,
For two bronze coins and pants of coarsest
　　　cloth,
To do the bidding of his seven mistresses,
And keep good watch over a thousand
　　　sheep.
Mistress Mara summoned folk all day,
The whole day, Saturday, she summoned
　　　folk
For the dance that would take place on
　　　Sunday,
To lure the shepherd Kokan from his sheep.
So, when the sun rose up that Sunday
　　　morning,
There came the shepherd Kokan from his
　　　sheep,
With his nine sheep-dogs trotting at his heel,
A hawthorn staff was balanced on his
　　　shoulder,
And from the staff a sack of ass-hide hung,
And in the sack a pair of roasted goats,
His pigtail poking through his wolfskin cap,
Two bristling bushes intertwined with it,
And dangling from each bush a little stack,

His toes all poking through his well-worn
    shoes,
His haunches shining brightly through
    his pants,
His kitty tumbling through the fold
    in front –
This kitty weighed three pounds and
    maybe more,
The pecker reached down to his knees,
    they saw!
As soon as he arrived he joined the dance
Next to his mistress Mara and two friends.
One of them said: "Let's give him
    underpants."
The other said: "No, no, let's watch instead."
But Mara said: "Now, Kokan, listen well,
I left your breakfast down below the field,
An omelette made with sixty eggs
    you'll find,
And thirty pounds or so of wholesome
    bread –
Tuck in, this snack should hold you till
    lunch comes!"
And Master Kokan hurried where she said,
And had a snack to hold him till lunch came,
And then returned to join the dance again.
He joined his mistress Mara in the ring,
His kitty tumbling through the fold before,

His pecker barely reached his knees,
        they saw.
Then Mara spoke out: "Master Kokan,
        hear this –
Tomorrow I shall pay the smith a visit,
Ask him to forge some armour for my cunt,
So that you may not have your way
        with me!"
And Kokan said: "Now hear this, Mistress
        Mara –
Tomorrow I shall go into the hills
To milk a thousand sheep and maybe more,
And twenty tubs I shall fill to the brim,
And for my prick's sake drink them
        to the dregs –
Nothing shall keep my pecker from your
        cunt!"
And then Kokan decided to get wed,
Two maidens' hands he asked for and
        he got,
He married Mara and Smiljana both,
And he placed Mara on a saddled horse,
But Smiljana a chestnut bareback rode,
Then Mara in her saddle spoke to him:
"My dearest man, now listen to me, please,
Raise my arse a little from the saddle,
So I may fart upon my family,
Fart on my aged father's long white beard,

My mother's cheese tub, brother's
      cabbage vat,
Because my brother's wife accuses me
Of shitting in their well – just think of it!
My sweet, upon my life I swear I didn't,
I shat a little to the side of it –
A crow just happened by and pecked the
      shit,
A pig just happened by and nudged the shit,
A dog just happened by and nosed the shit,
And so it was that half the shit fell in!"
Then Mistress Mara farted loud and clear,
And bits of saddle flew into the air,
And each piece hit one of the
      wedding guests,
Then the cross hit the best man in the chest.
And Kokan said: "You've grown so old,
      my love,
Days and years unnumbered now
      have passed!"
But Mara, in the saddle, said to him:
"Master Kokan, what do you mean by that,
No more than seven and seventy am I,
Seven and seventy is all I am!
And if you don't believe me you can ask
Young Smeljana, who was there at my birth,
And if you still do not believe, my sweet,
Then you can kiss my arse and eat my shit!"

Granny Todorina

Granny Todorina got up early
To call upon the shepherds for some wool.
Fate it was that then guided her footsteps
To a foolish shepherd named Zvekan.
When Zvekan saw Granny Todorina,
He set his bitch on her with all its fleas.
But Todorina reached between her buttocks,
Broke off a piece of shit and struck the bitch
So hard with it she didn't even twitch.
Zvekan the shepherd raged at her and swore:
"God strike you down, oh Granny Todorina,
You've killed my bitch and her
      with puppies too!"
But Granny Todorina spoke these words:
"Shepherd Zvekan, you'd better thank the Lord
Last night I waded through a puddle
Up to my waist, so that my shit got softer,
Or now your head would not be on your
      shoulders!"

Mummy's Milya

Mummy's Milya's pasturing the sheep,
Mother brings her girl a little snack:
Six or seven pounds of meaty beef,
Nine plump oaten loaves to go with it,
Corn bread weighing thirteen pounds or so,
And seven pounds of fragrant
        fart cheese too.
Then mummy's Milya to her mother said:
"Oh mother, what a light snack
        you have brought,
How shall I stop the sheep from
        straying then!"
And angrily she ran back to the house
And ate up everything she found at home.
Twelve ovenloads of bread was all she found,
Two oxen and two rams and
        two young goats,
But she devoured the patch of onions too,
And then, poor girl, she cried out
        in her hunger.
To wash it down she drank six kegs of wine,
Followed by four kegs of fiery brandy,
And after, three troughs overflowing
        with slops,
And then, poor girl, she cried out
        in her thirst,

So that her mother spoke to her and said:
"Oh, daughter mine, your faults are
        great indeed,
Who'll marry you with faults as great as these!"
Then like a swallow Milya bounded up,
Farted powerfully like a she-ass
That wanted terribly to piss and shit.
And when she pissed – the bitch,
        a pox upon her!
The waters flooded all the fields around,
Laying waste nine water-mills in their course,
And thirty wedding guests Old Nick had
        placed there
Could barely ford them even on their horses;
And when she shat – the bitch, a pox upon her!
She fertilized three fields that
        had been ploughed,
So that the wedding guests could barely cross
And many of their horses got bogged down.

Priest And Priest's Wife

What's the rumpus in the priestly
    household?
Joyful tidings, or some grave misfortune?
Neither joyful tidings, nor misfortune,
Just the priest admonishing his wife:
"Tell me, wife, whom did you do it with?"
"If you must know, it was with a merchant,
  And in exchange he gave me bronze and
    silver.
  I deaconed you, my husband, with the
    bronze,
  And with the silver made a priest of you!"
"So, do it, wife, with anyone you like,
  Then I shall be an archpriest in good time,
  And you may call yourself the archpriest's
    wife!"

Inat

Devojka se drugarici klela:
»Živ mi bratac, udati se neću
Ako l' kako silom nateraše,
Živ mi bratac, venčati se neću;
Ako l' kako silom nateraše,
Živ mi bratac, leći šnjime neću;
Ako l' kako silom nateraše
Živ mi bratac, metati mu ne dam;
Ako l' kako silom nateraše
Živ mi bratac, vaditi mu ne dam!«

Opklada momka i djevojke

Govorilo momče neženjeno,
govorilo lijepoj đevojci:
»Ođ', đevojko, da se opkladimo
u tvoj đerdan i u konja moga:
da jedinu noćcu prenoćimo,
da se jedno drugog ne mašino.«
Što rekoše, to i učiniše.
Kad je bilo oko polunoći,
al' govori lijepa đevojka:
»O junače, obrni se k meni –
mrtvoga te majka obrtala!
Zagrli me – usale ti ruke!
Poljubi me – istrula ti usta!
Ujedi me – ispali ti zubi!«

Mlad delija

Igra kolo nasred sela,
U kolu je mlad delija
Duga gunjca do pojasa,
Kratka kurca do koljenca.
Kad to viđ'li ljudi naši,
Vijećali, svijaćali,
Među sobom govorili:

»Na gunjac mu nastavite,
Od kurca mu ods'jecite!«
Kad to čule žene naše,
Ljudima su govorile:
»Od gunjca mu odrežite,
U kurac mu ne dirajte,
Sa glavom se ne igrajte!«

Nije trava

Devojčica ljubičicu brala,
Ubola je u pičicu trava –
Niji trava, već kurčeva glava!

Najbolje mjesto za selo

Ajde selo da selimo! –
Gdi ćemo ga naseliti? –
Međ' obrve devojačke. –
Tu ne može selo biti:
Nema šume, nema vode,
Nema zemlje za oranje!

Ajde selo da selimo! –
Gdi ćemo ga naseliti? –
Medu dojke devojačke. –
Tu ne može selo biti:
Nema šume, nema vode,
Nema zemlje za oranje!

Ajde selo da selimo! –
Gdi ćemo ga naseliti? –
Medu noge devojačke. –
Ta tu može selo biti:
Ima šume, ima vode,
Ima zemlje za oranje!

Djevojci

Oj devojko, srce moje,
Kad ti vidim sise tvoje,
Dreše mi se gaće moje.

Seka

Seka mete ulicu,
Natrćila guzicu,
Vidi joj se pika,
To je njojzi dika.

Ni raja ni kraja

Devojka se uz kurac penjala
Ne bi li se raja nagledala,
Ili raja ili kurcu kraja,
Desna joj se noga omaknula.
»Desna nono, jebeno ti deblo –
Bud s' omače, jer ne natače!«

Za Gajem

Posla mene mati
Za gaj drva brati;
Al' eto ti, mati,
Momče neženjeno,
Stade mene, mati,
Po trbuu klati
Ja mlidija, mati,
Učkur će mi dati;
Kad me sjede, mati,
Po pupčiću klati,
Ja mlidija, mati,
Pojas će mi dati;
Kad mi sjede, mati,
Noge podizati,

Ja mlidija, mati,
Mestve će mi dati;
A kad stade, mati,
U p-cu tiskati,
Ja mlidija, mati,
Oću umrijeti;
A kad sjede, mati,
Biser prosipati,
Ja mlidija, mati,
Da ću poletjeti!

Šta bi dala za junaka

Dala bi, dala
Dva konja vrana
Da ne spavam sama,
I trećega kulata
Za junaka kurata!

Nejaki Ranko

Sinoć majka oženila Ranka,
Ljuto kune udata devojka:
»Teško svakoj bednoj onoj majci
Koja daje jaku za nejaka –
Zora bela, a ja jošte cela!
Iz'o govno ko te oženio!
Diži noge, otpale ti ruke,
Vrane ti se na k-c osrale!«

Čudne štete

Čudne štete što je švale‍ ‍lete,
Pa se igra a ne zna da ljubi,
Tek se valja, pak mi suknju kalja,
Suknja bela od četir' karnera;
Mislila sam maramu navesti –
Kako ljubi – neće je poneti.

Ne može presti

Protužila skoro dovedena.
Da ne može presti nejebena. –
Ja je jeb'te, ja vodite majci,
Nek' je jebu materini znanci!

Snaša i brata

»Makni, snašo, guzovi!« –
»A ti, brato, brkovi!«

Čuđenje

Ja se čudim, ja se krstim
Kako pica vodu drži:
Ni obruča, ni daneta
Ni čestita zapušača;
Ja bi tamo pinter bio
Pa bi rupu zapušio.

Sve se čudim

Sve se čudim i krstim
Kako pica ne brsti,
No stala pa guli.
Poguli mi šljivice,
Jebem li joj vilice!

Poslije udaje

Dok sam bila devojčica mala,
Nisam znala ni pišati sama;
Fala Bogu, kad sam se udala,
Dignem nogu, sama voda curi!

Pop i djevojka

Pop đevojku uzeo za ruku,
Odveo je pod šupu na klupu,
Nabio joj ćelepuš na glavu,
Pa joj onda tijo besedio:
»Ja cu tebe za šmizlu povući,
Moj ce kurac sam u tebe ući!«

Čudan duhovnik

Moja majko, čudna duhovnika –
Povaljuje pa ispovijeda,
Noge diže, za griove pita!

Pod glogom

Posla mene moja mati
U lugove šumu brati.
Lugovi su obrodili
Gloginjami, zrninjami,
A ja jadna, vrlo gladna,
Ja se popeh da uberem.
Omače se noga s gloga,
Sa vrh gloga te pod glogom,
A pod glogom mlado momče.
Tek ja nad njim, on mi reče:
»Ko to na me jako kleče?«
U stid rekoh, pod njim legoh;
»Jahah tebe, sad ti mene!«

Prodaće livadu

U mog oca livada u ritu,
Prodaću je makar za vorintu,
Pa ću kupiť suknju lezi-dole,
I kecelju sama-skoči-gore,
I čarape svuci-pa-zatuci!

Gost

Svaka tica lepo poje –
Ali kos! Ali kos!
I domaćin dobro jebe –
Ali gost! Ali gost!

Nevolja

Kaluđeri travu kose među gorama,
Devojke im vodu nose među nogama:
»Ajte, oci, friške vode iz ladovine!«
Jedan prebi sebi kurac do polovine,
Pa ga nosi na kovače da ga pokuje –
Kovač kuca, a on puca, nuto nevolje!
Nosiše ga na zlatare da ga pozlate –
Zlatar zlati, kuro plati, nuto nevolje!
Nosiše ga na bajače da ga obaju –
Baba baje, kurac laje, nuto nevolje!
Nosiše ga na šlosere da ga okuje –
Šloser kuje, a on bljuje, nuto nevolje!

Kiselica

Da je meni pičke i paprike
Da načinim kurcu kiselice!

Fratar

Fratar pade sa međe,
Slomi kurac što jebe.
Skupiše se sve žene
I devojke vjerene:
»Jao, fratre, diko naša,
Po zlu pođe pizda naša!«

Majka i kći

»Jaoj, majko, kaluđer me budi,
On me budi, među oči ljubi!
Oću li ga poljubiti, majko?« –
»Ljubi, kćeri, ne bila prokleta!
Dok je majka tvoga doba bila,
Do zore je devet namirila
I desetog roditelja tvoga,
I otkala tropolu ponjavu!«

Ići će na pazar

Pička peče šarana,
Kurac gleda s tavana.
Uze pička lopatu,
Uđri kurca po vratu.
Stade kurac plakati,
A pička ga tješiti:
»Šuť, kurčiću, ne boj se,
Sutra jeste Vidovdan,
Ići ćemo na pazar,
Kupićemo svilen pas,
Zavićemo kurcu vrat!«

Huda komšinica

Svadila se pica i guzica,
Guza pici tijo besedila:
»Ao pico, uda komšinice,
Meni tvoji gosti dodijaše –
Tebe jebu, mene s mudi tuku!«

Tuđa Ljuba

Haj, huj, ne tuguj,
S tuđom ljubom ne druguj:
Tuđa ljuba golem vrag,
Slomiće ti kurcu vrat!

94

U gaju

Haj, haj, te u gaj –
Al' u gaju same daju!

Prepoznavanje po oku

Lako ti je seku znati
Koja misli pičke dati:
Samo gledaj koje oko
Na te gledi poširoko.

Molitva

Podaj, Boze, da mi dika može!

Bule i Vuk iz gorice

Podigle se bule na kopanje,
Ponijele pitu i pogaču
I bačvicu museleza vina,
Slatko pile, pak su i pospale.
Privuče se iz gorice Vuče,
Svakoj buli po dvaput zatuče.
Kad se bule od sna razabrale,
Al' govori begovica mlada:
»Aj, kadune, moje drugarice,
I prije smo museleza pile,
Al' nam nisu mokre gaće bile!
Da vadimo iz bačvice dugu,
Da mjerimo naše crne p. . .!«
One vade dugu iz kablice –
Svakoj buli p. . . od dvi duge,
Begovici od tri do četiri!

Starac i baba

Sitna kiša rominja,
Starac babu kominja
U livadi na kladi,
Teško starcu na babi!

Prijedlog

Oj snašice mila, ajde
Da od tebe pravim gajde,
Da ti pisak moj sateram
Samo dok se navečeram!

Opreznost

Smatrajući na pičicu
Kakvu ima komšinicu,
Moram, brate, u po noći
Otvoriti dobro oči:
Da kakogod pored rupe
Ne pogodim baš u dupe.

Za dukat

Piri vatru, jebi Katu!
Ne da Kata bez dukata;
Ja ću Kati dukat dati,
Pa ću Katu pojebati!
Podaj groš, jebi još,
Podaj dva, pa ću ja,
Podaj tri, pa ćeš ti!

Nevolja

Uh, žalosna, koliki je
Crven kurac u tog Mije!
Žalosnica njemu dati
Morala bi s' sva usrati!

Moja, drugo, to je ništa –
Da vi'š kakvog ima Pišta:
Kurčekanju sobom vuče,
Al' da ti ga još zavuče!

Snaša Vema

Zora sviti,
Još na kiti
Slatko drema
Snaša Vema.

Kovač i kovačica

Kovač kuje, kovačica prede,
U kovača gola muda glede.

I u starca

I u starca
Kao u jarca
Rep se kruti
Tušta puti,
Bubri žila
Ženi mila,
Prem ne često,
Ali čvrsto.

Uhvaćena

Ja posijah bob i dinje,
Navrani se đevojčica
Dinje brati, bob zobati.
Ja je čekah jednu večer,
Ja je čekah i dočekah,
Stavih ruku u njedarca,
U njedarca dva krastavca,
Nit' su zrela ni prezrela,
No najljevša za grizenja.

Stavih ruku malo niže,
Malo niže, niže pupka,
Ispod pupka dinja pukla,
A iz dinje voda teče,
Nagnah konja te napojih
I jedva se nje odvojih.

Kad svedu momka i djevojku
(U Dalmaciji i u Bosni)

Dobar veče, moj brajane,
Eto tebe vjerna ljuba –
Okreni je, moj brajane,
Prevrni je, moj brajane,
Dva-tri puta do zore
Da te braća ne kore!
Pred tobom je crna gora,
U gori je međedica,
Crnu kiku nadvjesila;
Ti potrgni bojno kopje,
Pa udari međedicu
Pod vilicu u resicu!
Vati joj se, moj brajane,
Vati joj se u njedarca,
Tu ćeš naći dva krastavca;
Vati joj se niže pupka
Tu ćeš naći – dinja pukla!

Momče i moma

Sadih jelu na planinu.
Navratih joj žubor-vodu;
Poslah momu da je čuva,
Ja mljah, čuvaće je;
Momu sanak boravio,
Poslah momče da je budi,
Ja mljah budiće je:
Podiže joj jednu nogu,
Ja mljah kopat' hoće;

Podiže joj drugu nogu,
Ja mljah orat' hoće;
Potrlja je po trbuhu,
Ja mljah valjat' hoće;
Podiže joj košuljicu,
Ja mljah barjak vije;
Odriješi gaćerine,
Ja mljah sijat' hoće;
Kad izvadi motovilo,
Ja mljah snovat' hoće.

Haranzade

Đevojka je platno bijelila
Na Sitnici na vodi studenoj.
Teke krpa, da s' osuši bila,
Tud naljeze momče Haranzada,
Te đevojci krpu pogazio.
Ona plače i kune ga ljuto:
»Da Bog da ti ljeto ne radilo!«
A momče joj riječ besjedilo,
A za brk se rukom uvatilo:
»Ovako mi često žito bilo,
Ne mogla mu naudit' godina!«
Al' đevojka viša Haranzada,
Pak se rukom za dojke vatila
I momčetu riječ besjedila:
»Ovaka ti krupa udarila,
Te sve tvoje žito polomila,
Ne mogla mu pomoći čestina!«
Tade momče besjedi đevojci,
A rukom se poniže vatio:
»Ovake mi klasutine bile,
Ne mogla im krupa nauditi!«
Al' đevojka viša Haranzada,
Poniže se rukom uvatila,
A momčetu tijo besjedila:
»Ovako ti s' čavke navadile,
Cijelo ti klasje proždirale?«

To rekoše, pak se potrpaše.

Kokan-čelebija

U z'o čas se Kokan pogodio,
U zle dane, u godine gladne,
Za dva groša i čakšire sukna
Da on služi sedam gazdarica
I da čuva iljadu ovaca.
Kolo kupi gazdarica Mara,
Kolo kupi vas dan u subotu,
A da igra vas dan u neđelju
Da domami Kokan' od ovaca.
Kad ujutro osvanu neđelja,
Al' eto ti Kokan' od ovaca,
Za njim kasa devetoro pasa,
Zavrg'o se drenovom batinom,
O batini jandžik od magarca
I u njemu dva pečena jarca,
Propao mu perčin kroz kalpaka,
Za perčinom do dva grma trnja,
Za svakijem naviljak sijena,
Porpali mu prsti kroz opanke
I obadva guza kroz čakšire,
Ispalo mi mače kroz rtmače –
Samo mu je mače od tri oke,
Kurac mu se do kljena kreće,
Od koljena baš nimalo neće!
Kako dođe, u kolo se vata
Baš do svoje gazdarice Mare
I još do nje dvije drugarice.
Jedna veli: »Da mu gaće damo!«
Druga veli: »Nemoj, da gledamo!«
Onda veli gazdarice Mara:
»Boga, tebe, Kokan-čelebija,
Ja sam tebi vruštuk ostavila
Tamo dolje niže kukuruza –
Kajgana je od šezdeset jaja
I pogača od trideset oka –

Srkni, kusni dok ti ručak dođe!«
I otide Kokane čobane,
Srknu, kusnu dok mu ručak dođe.
Opet dođe, u kolo se vata
Baš do svoje gazdarice Mare,
Ispalo mu mače kroz rtmače,
Kurčina se do koljena kreće,
Od koljena baš nimalo neće.
Onda veli gazdarice Mara:
»Boga tebi, Kokan-čelebija,
Idem sjutra jadna na kovače
Da sakujem oklope na pičku,
Pa mi ništa učiniti nećeš!«
Onda veli Kokan-čelebija:
»A da čuješ, gazdarice Maro,
Idem i ja sjutra u planinu
Da pomuzem hiljadu ovaca,
I namuzem dvadest čabrenica
I popijem uz kurčevo zdravlje –
Razbiću ti oklope na pički!«
I tu Kokan pođe se ženiti,
Pa isprosi do dvije đevojke,
Isprosio Maru i Smiljanu,
Pa povede Maru na samaru,
A Smiljanu na golu riđanu,
Onda veli Mara sa samara:
»Oj, Boga ti, da moj mili kume,
Izdigni mi dupe iz samara
Da poprdnem rodu na poodu,
Staru babu u bijelu bradu,
Mojoj majci u sirnu čabricu,
Milu bracu u kupusnu kacu,
Jer su mene snaje potvorile
Da sam im se u bunar posrala!
N'jesam, kume, života mi moga,
Već se posra ja više bunara –
Svraka dođe, kljuni, kume, govno,
Dođe prase, ćušni, kume, govno,
Dođe pseto, lapi, kume, govno,

Pola ga se u bunar prevali!«
A kad prde i poprde Mara,
Iskočiše štice iz samara,
Svaka štica svata udarila,
A krstina kuma po prsima.
Onda veli Kokan-čelebija:
»Al' si, jadna Maro, ostarila,
Izbrojila dane i godine!«
Onda veli Mara na samaru:
»O, Boga ti, Kokan-čelebija,
Kako sam ti jadna ostarila –
Sedamdeset i sedam godina,
Eto meni, bogme, više nema!
Ako li ti meni ne vjeruješ,
Ti upitaj Smiljane đevojke,
Koja mi je bila na babina;
Ako li mi ne vjeruješ, vojno,
Izjedi mi iz guzice govno!«

Baba Todorina

Poranila Baba Todorina
Međ' čobane da vune poprosi.
Namera je beše namerila
Na nekakva Zvekana čobana.
Kad je Zvekan babu opazio,
On je na nju vaške napujkao.
Al' se maša baba međ guzove
Pa otkida brabonjak od guza,
Te udara kuju Zvekanovu.
Kako ju je lako udarila,
Nije kuja ni repom vinula.
Ljuto kune Zvekane čobane:
»Bog t' ubio, baba Todorina,
Gdi mi ubi kučku od štenaca!«
Al' besedi baba Todorina:
»Mol' se Boga, Zvekane čobane,
Što sam sinoć baru pregazila
Te su meni odmekli brabonjci,

Sam se ne bi nanosio glave!«

Milja materina

Ovce pasla Milja materina,
Za njom majka užinu prinaša:
Sedam oka goveđine mesa,
Prinosila devet ovsenica,
I dvanaest oka mlaćenica
I šest oka sira prdenjaka.
Onda veli Milja materina:
»Jao, majko, lagane užine,
Kako ću ti ići za ovcama!«
Ražljuti se, pa oskaka dvoru,
Sve izjede što kod dvora nađe,
Samo ljeba dvanaest vuruna,
I još do dva vola bikovita,
I još do dva ovna škuljevita,
I dva mlada jarca prčevita,
I izjede punu bašcu luka,
I još jadna sve od gladi kuka,
I popila šest akova vina,
I četiri žežene rakije,
I popila tri kabline meće
I još jadna sve kuka od žeđe!
Onda joj je majka besjedila:
»Ćeri moja, teške su ti rane,
Kogod čuje uzeti te neće!«
Skoči Milja kako lastavica,
Kučka prde kako magarica,
Ljuto Milji pišati prituži,
A kad pišnu, pas joj jebo majku,
Ode voda preko svega polja
I obori devet vodenica;
Vrag nanese trideset svatova,
Te na konj'ma jedva preplivaše;
Kad se posra, da joj jebem majku,
Tri je njive ona nagnojila,
Jadva svati na konj'ma prejaše

I konji se mlogi zaglibiše.

Pop i popadija

Kakva j' kavga u popovu dvoru –
Al' je radost al' velika žalost? –
Nit' je radost nit' velika žalost,
Nego popo svoju pošu kara:
»Kaži, pošo, kome jesi dala?« –
»Dala jesam jednom butigaru,
Dao mi je groše i dukate –
S groši jesam tebe đakonila,
A s dukati tebe zapopila!« –
»Podaj, pošo, kome tebi drago,
Ne bi li me protom učinila,
Ne bi li se protinica zvala!«

Audrey Jones

Illustrator's Afterword

Illustration is itself a form of translation, especially where poetry is concerned. A visual image can be developed from the mood, the content, specific descriptions of things or actions, but since the illustration cannot replicate the poem as a whole, it is necessary to invent a parallel conceptual framework in which the visual response has a self-consistent integrity to match that of the stimulus, which is a verbal one. To put it another way, the representation of any concrete objects referred to in a poem has to be arranged so that their articulation in some way (not necessarily always the same way) resembles either the articulation of the parts of the poem or the possible phases of response. In the best of all worlds, an illustration could achieve both, without closing off other possible interpretations.

Of course, unlike a verbal language-to-language translation, the visual translation can be "read" at the same time as the original version, because it is seen in a different way. The visual immediacy of a picture's presence on a page will inevitably affect the first response to the poem itself. It might even influence subsequent readings, either in positive or adverse ways; this puts the illustrator in a difficult, if interesting, position. I did not write, collect or translate (in the verbal sense) the poems in question; but in translating them from the verbal to the visual mode, I had to take into account the fact that my work would have a primary impact on the eye, and that the innate differences in effect between the visual and verbal meant that whatever I did, it would result in something very different in appearance from a parallel text.

When it was first suggested to me that I might provide illustrations for these poems, I was interested and also curious about what they could possibly be like. When I was given the actual texts to read, I had two immediate reactions: first, that I did not want to treat them as "curiosities", and secondly, that their sexual content was going to make it difficult to find appropriate images. However, when I first read the poems, I was struck most of all by the humour. In many cases, the humour of the situations evoked seems to be much more interesting than the sexual outcome. It is true that many of the poems are very direct about sexual organs and the processes of excretion, and so on, but the general feeling is not really erotic. Rude, certainly. But to a large extent, ridiculous – I felt there was a sense of ridicule, not just of the sexual acts, but of the listener, a question of how far can you go?

When I started focusing on the sexual angle, however, and its apparent challenge – how far could I go? – not only did there not seem to be any visual precedents on which I could draw for assistance, but I was put in the position of having to think primarily of stylistic solutions. I thought of, and discarded, various options, but could not find a satisfactory way to deal with the subject, until I realised that the problem had been created precisely by seeing the sexual material as the main topic. To do this was to put the poems in a historical vacuum. I had to look at the content of the poems in another way.

It became clear that some of the poems were simply impossible to illustrate, since they worked in a purely verbal way – jokes, or insults, or prayers, which did not suggest anything specifically visual. (One of the poems is a joke which, in an almost identical version, I heard in London about three years ago!) The only way to deal with these would be some form of abstraction, an option I had already discarded on the grounds that it would be at odds with the nature of the material and impose a predetermined expressionism on the words. I also thought it would look like an evasive tactic in relation to the sexual content.

On the other hand, there were several poems which provided a very definite visual stimulus, and I decided to start with these, to draw the people and the objects, to make the circumstances as concrete as possible and to let the sexuality emerge from that.

I decided it would be best to make the illustrations very clear so as to suggest a real historical context. I also needed to find an equivalent for the humour, since verbal and visual jokes do not work in quite the same way.

As I began to work, I also began to realise that explicit representations of sexual organs or intercourse would create a feeling quite different from that evoked by reading about them. Whether or not a modern audience would regard them as pornographic or obscene, it appeared to me that to make the drawings overtly sexual would be ahistorical in two ways. In the first place, I could not believe that the originators of these poems would ever have seen pictures of such a kind, or found them acceptable if they had, and while I certainly didn't want to produce pastiche "ethnic" drawings, neither did I want to create illustrations which would in some way work against the mood of the poems. In the second place, I did in fact do a draft for the poem "Gathering Wood" which showed a man with an erect penis, but I found it difficult to do this without reducing the clothing to a stylised minimum, and thus the figures became generalised in a kind of sub-classical way. In other words, since much of the sex seems to occur when the participants are at least partly clothed, and I assume that the clothing was quite bulky, in the way of peasant costume, there really wouldn't be much to see. I could either distort the costume, which would lose the sense of a particular time and place, or I would be left with pictures of entangled clothes, in which case the drawings would all be extremely similar, thus losing the differences of tone in the poems themselves. The only way to resolve the latter problem would have been to invent something like Japanese erotica, in which a great deal of attention is paid to the disposition of clothing in relation to particular sexual activities: this did not seem to me to be at all appropriate!

Once I began to concentrate on what there was in the way of specifically visual reference, it became apparent that many of the poems belonged to traditions which were already familiar, in a broad sense, from European folk myths, fairy tales and so on. The narratives of confrontation, boasting, metamorphosis, mysterious and unaccountable sexual happenings, could all be traced in one form or another. (The poem "Mother and Daughter" could even be read as a peasant version of Penelope and her weaving; I was utterly charmed by the idea of the rug!) I was myself quite surprised when these elements emerged, so I do not feel I was imposing predetermined structures on the material. To some extent, I felt I was undergoing a process analogous to, or perhaps the reverse of, Robert Graves' accounts of possible iconographic mis-reading.

Having said this, I also thought it important that no-one reading the book should think I had not represented the sexual act in detail because I was in some way afraid of doing so, whether for reasons of prudery or publication. The clarity of the images therefore has an additional purpose: it is intended to depict particular circumstances which can themselves convey a sexual charge. I hope this is suggestive without being in any way lubricious. This approach made it possible for me to refer to my memory of images which had various kinds of underlying sexual connotations, where the style as well as the content might be suggestive, such as the fairy story element in "Underneath the Hawthorn" which reminded me of the illustrations in nineteenth century children's books, in particular the Andrew Lang Fairy Books. At the same time, any story about a girl, some fruit, a tree, and falling, needs a snake.

There are two illustrations which are necessarily and intentionally sexual: "Red Knight" and "Astonished". The first was a relatively simple matter to illustrate – the convoluted triple image of the helmeted saint, spear and the serpent are quite familiar from religious imagery, especially in the Eastern Church, and I am sure that the poem carries an awareness of this image. St George in particular is a much more important saint in Eastern Europe than in the West, despite being the patron saint of England. The second was diabolically difficult – the poem consists entirely of negative imagery, which is of course predictable, given the subject. (Although I was interested in the fact that in "The Turkish Women and Vuk from the Woods", the woman with the highest rank, the bey's young wife, is deemed to have the largest internal size. In our culture, esteem is awarded to women with large exterior but small interior sexual parts.) In the end, the result was a kind of Zen joke. I hope that this, as well as the other illustrations, help to provide some interesting ways of reading the poems.

Translation is sometimes taken for granted as a procedure which automatically reproduces something by copying it; to some extent this is particularly true of visual translation, since its physical presence can affect the viewer without apparent reciprocal effort. I would like to think that in this book the verbal and visual modes counterpoint each other, and that their interaction makes apparent the various possibilities open to the translator. Illustration, like illumination, is intended to clarify, to shed light, and perhaps even to enlighten.

Daniel Weissbort

Translator's Afterword

It remains only for me to add a note on the transla-
tors' procedure. Since I have a reading knowledge
of another Slavic language, Russian, and since Serbo-
Croatian is pronounced as it is written, I was able,
with Toma Longinovic's help, to pick my way
through the Serbo-Croatian script, to own the songs
insofar as a stranger can be said to do so. Actually
had I not been able to enter quite so happily into the
texts, I doubt whether I would have been able,
under the circumstances (a regular teaching semes-
ter, following a serious illness), to bring my work to
a conclusion. (Of course, as we know, a translation
is never finished, only abandoned.)

So, first we made a photocopy of the entire
collection for my use. Then we started at the be-
ginning. Toma Longinovic read the poems aloud,
selecting those he thought to be translatable, that is:
not entirely dependent on sound. Often he would
exclaim appreciatively before reading a poem, thus
engaging my attention; sometimes his reading
would be rather discursive; at other times, he was
more declamatory, emphasizing the rhythm, the
comical or often grotesque acoustic patterns, the
texture of end-, internal- and initial-rhymes, asso-
nance and alliteration; frequently ·he broke into
laughter; at the end, he would generally make some
comment....I mention all this, because it was through

his eyes and ears, through his spontaneous reactions, his impromptu remarks, that I first experienced the poems. His uninhibited delight in this surprising part of his native culture was communicated to me, without which I should probably not have got further than a literal transcription.

After Toma Longinovic had read a poem in the original Serbian, after we had savoured it and I had got some idea of its meaning from his comments and from my recognition of certain Slavic roots, he would dictate a word-for-word translation, which I jotted down alongside or under the source text. While the poem was still ringing in my ear, I would question him and try out various words and phrases that came to mind. (This was only the first stage and there were frequent consultations later. However, my point is that this initial assault was vital, the energizing basis for everything that followed.) We laughed a lot too. But so bawdy and ribald was much of the material that, even as we laughed together and I scribbled down the provisional translations, I wondered whether I could summon the language for it. Being a native Britisher of the middle-classes, raised in London, in the '40s and '50s, on BBC English, I was not quite at home, even after more than a decade in the United States, with American diction, which often seems more racy or casual. However, so pleasurable was the reading of these poems that I was spurred on. Here I must add that Toma Longinovic's English often included whole lines which I felt sure should be preserved in a "final" version. Interestingly, though English is a second language for him, his feeling, as an immigrant, for the American idiom was more authentic than mine. I wish I could have preserved more of his easy way with words.

The present collection leaves out a little over a half of the contents of the original book. However, many of the poems we discarded were very short, fragmentary, whereas we did translate all of the longer, narrative poems. We would read ten or fifteen poems at a time, and I'd work on these, until I had produced two or three drafts of each. Then we'd move on to the next ten or fifteen. It was clear from the start that, while there was a good deal of formulaic repetition or parallelism, which was more or less reproducible, the often quite elaborate and comical sound effects were another matter. And yet if something were not done about this, what would be left? In his introduction to *The Popular Songs of Serbia* (1824), Vuk Karadžić wrote: "They [the women's songs] are sung conversationally, while the heroic songs are sung for others to listen to, and so singing is more important than the song in women's songs, while it is the reverse with heroic songs." What I take this to mean is that the women's songs were a ritualized expression of the day-to-day commerce between villagers, in the performance of which all participated, whereas the "heroic songs" were declaimed by a specialized "singer of songs" to a listening (generally all-male) audience. In the latter, the narrative element was foregrounded, whereas the former were more a matter of gesture, as it were, vocalized. It followed that, if I was to do more than merely provide a semantic crib, I should have to convey something of the gusto, the melodic and metric vitality, of the songs. Of course, I wanted to do both, and in the event I compromised. But the compromise rarely, if ever, led me (knowingly) to distort or alter the original meaning – I preferred to abandon the translation, if this seemed to be happening. That is, I rejected literalism and also resisted the temptation (admittedly, never very great) to "imitate" the poems, to re-work them in some modern, more familiar, idiom and ambience, the reason being that I did not feel such a drastic expedient to be necessary. Probably, this is because the songs themselves are so timeless, rooted, as Toma Longinovic suggests, in our common pagan heritage – which gives the blasphemies and even obscenities an almost sacramental weight!

A word about the metre. Many of these pieces, and all the long ones at the end, are in decasyllabics (tending to the trochaic). Rather than apply our native iambic pentameter, I opted (though not in every case) for a fairly loose decasyllabic line, not insisting on the iambic pace. But even though I counted syllables rather than stresses in the early drafts, I ended up, of course, mostly with iambic lines. However, I like to think that this strategy allowed me to be more flexible, to preserve something of the spoken quality of the verse. I also generally respected the lack of enjambment, characteristic of oral poetry.

A few examples will illustrate how these English versions came about. Take "How Can She Spin?" (page 36). Toma Longinovic's word-for-word is as follows:

> The newly wed is complaining.
> She cannot spin if she is not screwed.
> Either fuck her or take her to her mother,
> Let her mother's acquaintance fuck her!

The final version is:

> The new bride makes a fearful din:
> If she's not screwed, how can she spin!
> Either fuck her or take her home to mother,
> Let her mama's lover fuck her!

The lines are decasyllabic and rhyme aabb, the bb rhyme being approximate (*majci/znaci*). I did not preserve the decasyllabic line here, but in such a small piece it seemed more important to concentrate on finding at least one strongly rhyming pair, hence my somewhat hyperbolical "makes a fearful din", and I ended up with three eight-syllable lines, octosyllabics also being typical of Yugoslav folk poetry. The opportunity presented itself, as well, to introduce a conceit (screw/spin), since Toma Longinovic used the word, "screwed" instead of "fucked", even though the Serbo-Croatian *jebena* would normally be translated as "fucked". This fortuitously suggests a connection between the bride's reluctance or inability to work at the spinning-wheel and her not being properly served, or wound up, by her husband; I was delighted to have been made a present of it. My bb rhymes are more slanted than the Serbian, but this is oral poetry and I felt the assonance was sufficient – just about! Here, too, my co-translator's ad verbum interpretation provided me with an attractive enough solution, though (perversely?) I tried one or two others before returning to it. In other words, this poem was more or less a gift.

Another example, perhaps not quite typical – here I allowed a convenient and (I hope) amusing rhyme to lead me somewhat further away from the strict literal sense – is "The Friar" (page 53). Toma Longinovic's word-for-word is as follows:

> The monk fell on the field,
> And broke the prick that fucks.
> All the wives gathered
> And betrothed girls:
> "Ouch, brother (or monk), our pride (or glory),
> Here is trouble for our cunts!"

The rhyme is aabbcc, the cc rhyme being homophonous, though the penultimate words, too, echo each other (*diko nasa/pizda nasa*). In addition, the last line is quite strongly alliterated (*Po zlu pode pizda nasa*) making it more emphatic and even petulant-sounding - at least to my ears! The aabb rhymes, it should be added, may also be read as aaaa (*mede/jebe/zene/vjerene*), putting still more pressure on the final couplet, which is in any case set off, being speech. While I tinkered for quite a while with the first four lines, the final couplet occurred to me almost at once. However, I tried to find an alternative, since I was afraid that it might sound too clever – or perhaps too facile! Furthermore, Toma Longinovic's rendering of the unobtrusive little Serbian colloquialism ("Here is trouble") possessed, it seemed to me, intrinsic comic merits. An early version went: "The friar fell upon

117

the field" [shades of battle rather than rusticity]/
"And broke the prick he was wont to wield." [Ugh!
Apart from finding a rhyme for "field", I didn't
know what to do about the utterly uncompromis-
ing "The prick that fucks", and somehow – perhaps
due to embarrassment? – I went in the opposite
direction]/"The village wives all gathered round
him/And the girls who were betrothed. My latest
version is:

> The friar tripped on a sod and fell.
> He broke the prick that fucks so well.
> Married or betrothed, the women
> Gathered round and stared at him:
> "Oh, our cunts' pride, oh holy friar,
> Is this a sign of heaven's ire!"

In my revision, that is, I tried to restore both the
village note ("tripped on a sod", though perhaps it
has become slightly slapstick in the process), as
well as (somewhat) the frank description of the
prick. I made several attempts at a bb rhyme but
opted in the end for the unrhyming, but echoing
"women/at him", and I left the concluding couplet,
since it provided at least an appropriate sense of
finality, even if it was, perhaps, rather high-flown.

In another, very short poem, "Oh, The Guest!"
(page 50), the highly elliptical nature of the source
text could not be captured in the translation, which,
however, even in its more relaxed form, seems to
work sufficiently well. (The same was not true of a
number of other tiny poems, depending almost
wholly on playfulness of sound, rather than on
semantic content. See below.) Toma Longinovic's
word-for-word is as follows:

Every bird sings nicely –
But blackbird! But blackbird!
And the host fucks well –
But guest! But guest!

He added afterwards that the even lines were com-
pressions of: "But the blackbird is best" and "But
the guest is best". As the poem rhymes abab, he had
handed me the bb rhyme ("best"/"guest") on a
platter! My version is:

Every bird sings sweetly –
But blackbird's best! Blackbird's best!
And the host fucks featly –
But, oh, the guest! Oh, the guest!

I had no regrets about substituting "sweetly" for
"nicely", since "nicely" is a colourless word in
English. On the other hand, I certainly hesitated
over "featly"; but then I decided to go ahead, partly
on account of the parallel alliteration ("sings
sweetly"/"fucks featly"). Perhaps this compen-
sates a little for the loss of a different kind of
parallelism in lines two and four of the original (*Ali
kos! Ali kos!/Ali gost! Ali gost!*). In any case,
"sweetly" and "featly" are both somewhat archaic
or Romantic terms, and so of a piece. Even if the
diction here is a little out of keeping with that of the
rest of the collection, I felt that "featly" was eccen-
tric enough to be acceptable in this context! (An
alternative to "featly" might be "neatly", but that
word suffers from overuse in contemporary youth
slang.) To sum up, I have from time to time taken
advantage – as most translators do – of certain
opportunities that presented themselves in Eng-
lish, allowing me to compensate for inevitable losses.

"For A Ducat" (page 67), a slightly longer poem, will serve as a final example. Toma Longinovic's word-for-word is as follows:

Fan the fire, fuck Kata!
Kata doesn't give without ducat;
I will give a ducat to Kata,
And I will fuck Kata!
Give a grosh, fuck more,
Give two, I will fuck too,
Give three, and you will too!

My final version was:

Sweep the chimney, flames go up it,
Kate won't fuck without a ducat.
Here's one ducat for my Kata,
Now I'm sure she'll let me fuck her!
Give her two, she'll fuck you,
Give her three, she'll fuck me,
Give her four, she'll fuck more!

A glance at the original shows how dependent this little jingle is on internal rhyming and a very concentrated range of vowel sounds, as well as alliteration:

Piri vatru, jebi Katu!
Ne da Kata bez dukata;
Ja ću Kati dukat dati,
Pa ću Katu pojebati!
Podaj groš, jebi još,
Podaj dva, pa ću ja,
Podaj tri, pa ćeš ti!

Fortunately, the main rhyming words (*Kata, dukat, jebati* / "Kate" or "Kata", "ducat", "fuck") straddle both languages, without which, of course, it would be impossible to render the poem even as approximately as is done here. Acoustically, as well as semantically, the poem divides into two parts, lines

1-4 and 5-7. It was important to preserve this division, the deceleration brought about by a more marked caesura in each of the last three lines producing the effect of a coda. I suppose I am least happy with my first line: "Sweep the chimney, flames go up it", since with "chimney" we move outside the phonetic range. However, as this comes right at the start, I reckoned that at least it was not interrupting the flow once it got under way. Another problem was the *dukat*, indispensable for the rhyme scheme, unless I was going to Americanize the poem by using a "buck/fuck" type of rhyme. In fact, I tried out a version mixing Americanisms and Britishisms: "Poke the fire and the flames go higher,/ But Kate won't fuck without bucks,/I'll give Catherine some brass,/Now I'm sure she'll move her arse!/Give her two bucks, she'll fuck you Jack,/ Give her three, again it's me!" Even supposing this dreadful version could have been somewhat improved, it seemed too much of a cultural hotchpotch, out of phase with the rest of the translations, moving clumsily towards "imitation". When the slant rhymes, "Kata/fuck her" and "ducat/up it", occurred to me, it clinched matters. "Chimney" still bothers me, but at least it has obvious sexual connotations. Ducat? Well, even though the word may be unfamiliar to some, it has the right Austro-Hungarian or Central European associations. The "grosh", I felt, could be dispensed with, particularly as a rhyme was readily available without it and the last three lines of the translation were even more unified than in the original Serbian.

Probably this is sufficient to give the reader some sense of how the poems here relate to the source texts. There were a number of minimal jingles that either defeated me or kept me at arm's length. One such goes:*Žaba kreknu*, ("Frog croaks,")/ *Maj zabreknu*; ("Mine grows bigger;")/ *Pile pisnu*, ("Chicken chirps,") *Maj ti tisnu*; ("Mine went in;" / *Gavan gaknu*, ("Raven caws,")/*Maj ti taknu!* ("Mine goes in!") My last-ditch attempt was: "Frog croaks,/ Mine soaks;/Crow caws,/Mine saws;/Chicken chirps,/Mine burps!" The imagery, such as it is (the "sawing" of sexual intercourse, pre-climactic emissions?), is too literary, or too arbitrary. Nor did any way of rendering the following occur to me: *Ova seka do meneka* ("The girl next to me")/*Iste mesa od meneka* – ("Asks meat from me –")/*Ja imado pajoj dado!* ("I had some and I gave her!") Nor this one: *Mala seka* ("Little girl")/*Do meneka* ("Next to me")/ *Guz sevelji*, ("Moves her buttocks,")/*Mre u zelji* ("Dies with Desire")/*Da se baci* ("For me to fuck her")/*Nakitaci!* ("Puts herself in position!"). This last verse, and others like it, would seem to relate to the *kolo* or round-dance, itself possibly a survival of pre-Christian fertility rituals (see Toma Longinovic's introduction).

The longer poems, with which this collection concludes, have more narrative content than the other pieces. I have tried, on the whole, to preserve the decasyllabic line of the folk epics – or, as here, mock-epics. The originals rhyme only intermittently (usually for dramatic effect), and this too has, for the most part, been reproduced in the English.

Here, the meaning or story, rather than the form or sound, is what matters most, and the translations are lexically somewhat closer to the source texts.

If the poems in this volume seem too literary, it is perhaps inevitable, given that I was not prepared, or able, to translate them into a more informal dialect than the one which, for better or worse, is my own. Nor did I feel nearly sure enough of myself to attempt the kind of ethnopoetic re-creations that some translators of Native American songs, for example, have tried. It was nevertheless immense fun to work with these songs, and I hope that some of that fun has come across. The comic muse is at least as present here as the erotic one!

(1984)

Postscript

As I re-read my "Afterword", some years after writing it, a parenthetical remark in the first paragraph, referring to a "serious illness", seems to need amplifying. The illness in question was cancer, and I was recuperating from radical surgery of the jaw. Though the prognosis was relatively good, I could not, of course, be given a clean bill of health right away. It has since become clear to me that the women's songs contributed, in some measure, to my recovery. Strange as this may seem, the intimate contact (implicit in translation) enabled me to draw on the primitive or elemental forces that inhabit them. As any "victim" of cancer knows, anxiety, depression, outrage, denial, are only a few of the negative feelings that inhibit recovery. Translating the women's songs gave me access to a certain élan vital. Though I was only dimly aware of it at the time, I believe it may be said that, in a sense, I actually participated in the life-enhancing rites Toma Longinovic discusses in his introduction! (I am not, of course, claiming a special status for the translations themselves, the reader being their sole judge.)

Life-threatening illness has its privileges, and so, finally, I join with my co-translator in expressing the hope that the "heroic" pretensions of so many of today's political leaders of Yugoslavia (and not just Yugoslavia) will be tempered by the "irreverent" spirit that informs songs, such as those presented here. After all, we reject the Goddess at a terrible risk! My comradely thanks, then, to Tomislav Longinovic, who made the work possible and to Audrey Jones whose illustrations contextualise these songs in a way that only illustrations can. To Translation herself, my reverent thanks...

BIOGRAPHICAL NOTES

Charles Simic was born in Yugoslavia in 1938, coming to the United States in 1949. Poet, essayist, and translator, he has published 15 collections of his own work, including *The World Doesn't End*, for which he was awarded the 1990 Pulitzer Prize for Poetry. His most recent volume of poems is *The Book of Gods and Devils*. Mr Simic is also the author of *Wonderful Words, Silent Truth: Essays on Poetry and a Memoir*. Among numerous awards, he has received two P.E.N. International Prizes for his translations of Serbo-Croatian, South American and French poetry. He is a professor of English at the University of New Hampshire.

Daniel Weissbort, London born, half-emigrated to the United States around 1975. He is now a professor of English and Comparative Literature at the University of Iowa, where he directs the Iowa Translation Workshop. Besides three volumes of his own poetry and, most recently, a Northern House pamphlet *Fathers*, Weissbort has published a number of translations of poetry and prose, mostly from French and Russian. He has edited *Post-War Russian Poetry* and the recently published *The Poetry of Survival: Post-War Poets of Easter and Central Europe*, as well as a collection of papers: *Translating Poetry: The Double Labyrinth* . In 1965, with Ted Hughes, Weissbort founded the magazine Modern Poetry in Translation.

Tomislav Longinovic was born in Yugoslavia and came to the United States as a member of the University of Iowa's International Writing Program. A graduate of the Writers Workshop of the University of Iowa, where he also earned a doctorate in Comparative Literature, Longinovic is now a professor in the Slavic Department of the University of Wisconsin, in Maddison. His novel *Moments of Silence* was published by Burning Books, San Francisco. The University of Arkansas Press will publish his critical study of the contemporary Slavic novel, *Slavic Margins*.

Audrey Jones lives in London. She was educated at the Slade School, the University of Essex and the Courtauld Institute. She taught History of Art for several years at Camberwell and St Martin's Schools of Art, where her particular fields were the Renaissance, History of Drawing, and other subjects in complementary studies. Since 1980 she has been a full-time painter, and has sold a number of paintings to private collectors, some of them commissioned works and portraits. Among other things, she is currently working on a visual diary.